Woman of God®

Living Loved

Gail Marsh

His Message. Your Mission.

Devotions for Women

The mission of CTA is
to glorify God by providing purposeful products
that lift up and encourage the body of Christ—
because we love him.

Woman
of God®
Living Loved

Gail Marsh

Copyright © 2017 CTA, Inc.
1625 Larkin Williams Rd.
Fenton, MO 63026

www.CTAinc.com

ISBN 978-1-943216-19-2
PRINTED IN THAILAND

Woman of God®

Living Loved

> I have loved you with an everlasting love.
> *Jeremiah 31:3*

How do you introduce yourself? Do you follow your name with a few details about where you work? Or where you used to work? Or where you would like to work someday? If so, you're like most people. Who you are in our society is often defined by what you do.

During the coming week, we'll take a closer look at you—who you are and what you do—in light of Jeremiah 31:3. We'll consider God's amazing interaction with you as a Woman of God: Living Loved.

Love You More!

> *I have loved you with an everlasting love.*
> **Jeremiah 31:3**

At first glance, the sign seemed a bit strange. I was shopping for the perfect wedding gift when I spotted the exquisitely framed art. It hung at the very top of the department store's wedding gift display and seemed to dwarf the gifts displayed below it. The gold-leaf block letters stretched from one edge of the frame to the other, side to side and top to bottom. They proclaimed, "Love you more!" I did a double take, reading again: "Love you more!"

Think about the words *Love you more!* in light of Jeremiah 31:3. Who is speaking these words? It's God himself! The same God who called the entire universe into being. "Let there be . . .," he said. And it was. That's the one who loves you! The same God who crafts each child's smile, dimples and all. That one—that one, true God—loves you!

God loves you with all his might. He never started loving you. He has loved you forever, and he claims you as his very own. He will fight for you. He will defend you. He will comfort you. All this because you belong to him. God loves you. Yes, you!

And he is truly the only one who can legitimately proclaim: "Love you more!"

God is the best, the champion, at loving. That's because "God is love" (1 John 4:8). God's very nature is love—heartfelt, powerful, genuine love. Love is who God is! And he alone enables us truly to love, to love him and to love one another. What's more, when we fail to imitate God's perfect love, he forgives us—completely.

God's greatest act of love came to earth wrapped in strips of cloth and lying in a manger. Jesus, God's own dear Son, loved us to death—his own—even when we were sinful and totally unlovable. The Bible says:

God shows his love for us in that while we were still sinners, Christ died for us. Romans 5:8

"Love you more!" God reminds us. No matter what happened yesterday, regardless of what happens today or tomorrow, you can be sure his infinite love will hold you close, now and forever!

Lord, I am so humbled by your love. Remind me of it continually today, especially when . . .

Transformed!

> *I have loved you with an everlasting love.*
> *Jeremiah 31:3*

Which invention introduced during your lifetime has changed your life the most? Laptop computers? Cell phones? Debit cards? Cable TV? GPS systems? Online shopping?

Inventions transform lives and have been doing so since the development of the wheel. Some may argue that many ideas originally intended to simplify life have made it even more complicated. Still, we have to agree that our lives are definitely affected, transformed even, by the inventions of the past few decades.

Our technological advances may be impressive, but God has been transforming lives in even more impressive ways since the dawn of time. God's love changes things!

Remember Matthew, the tax collector? It's likely that Matthew got as rich as he was by cheating others. Those who collected taxes for the Roman government did not receive a salary. Instead, they were allowed to add a fee on to the taxes they collected. These fees were never small. If anyone objected, the tax collector could call on local Roman legions to make a collection call.

Matthew probably had few friends, but he had his money and his power. He was willing to settle for that. He was willing, that is, until Jesus offered Matthew more, more than anyone else ever had or ever could have. Jesus offered Matthew God's unconditional love and acceptance.

Realizing it, Matthew jumped up from his tax table and walked away, leaving his former life behind. He traded in his tax collecting job to follow Jesus, who at the time was a little-known, itinerant teacher. Jesus' love changed Matthew. Forever. That's powerful, transformational love!

Or consider Saul of Tarsus. Intent on eliminating the cult of Christ-followers, Saul methodically persecuted the followers of "The Way," jailing some, killing others. Then, Jesus intervened, appearing to Saul in a vision on the road to Damascus.

Jesus intervened, offering forgiveness, acceptance, and yes, genuine, powerful love. That love transformed Saul as it had transformed Matthew before him. Saul the persecutor became Paul the apostle.

The power of God's love, in Christ, is at work in you today. It's true! And here's God's promise to you:

He who began a good work in you will bring it to completion at the day of Jesus Christ.
Philippians 1:6

Lord God, sometimes I forget how fiercely you love me. Remind me . . .

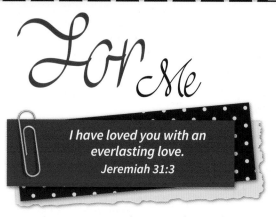

I have loved you with an everlasting love.
Jeremiah 31:3

> Jesus loves us, this we know.
> For the Bible tells us so.

That doesn't sound quite right, does it? The words *us* and *we* don't belong in the original lyrics. The words actually read like this:

> Jesus loves me, this I know.
> For the Bible tells me so.

The little personal pronoun *me* makes a huge difference, doesn't it? The author of this beloved children's hymn understood Jesus' love. She recognized that Jesus' love is personal. Yes, it's true that God loves all people, from everywhere and every era. But Jesus' love makes a much greater impact on us. It carries a vastly deeper meaning because we know that love is personal.

God's love is personal, because it's relational:

When the fullness of time had come, God sent forth his Son, born of woman, born under the law, to redeem those who were under the law, so that we might receive adoption as sons. Galatians 4:4–5

God's love, in Jesus, brings each one of us into his family. Not as distant cousins or as in-laws or extended family members. No. We are adopted as heirs and cherished as dear daughters of the Most High. God's love draws us close and keeps us secure in much the same way as a loving father embraces his own child.

God's love for you, in Jesus, is also intimate. Your heavenly father loves you because he knows you—really knows you. He created you. Consider:

Even the hairs of your head are all numbered. Luke 12:7

Before I formed you in the womb I knew you. Jeremiah 1:5

The unique, intimate love that God has for you is real. Yes, he knows your sins—even the ones you keep hidden from others. He knows them because he died for them. In the cross, he forgives you and loves you still.

God's personal and intimate love for you is also fiercely protective. Jesus says:

I know my own and my own know me. John 10:14

Your Warrior-Shepherd, Jesus, stands ready to fight for you. He'll do whatever it takes to keep you close to himself. His love is stronger than anything that frightens you, and you can be sure his love for you will never end. That's love! Real love!

Thank you, God, for loving me. Help me reflect your love today . . .

Guaranteed

> **I have loved you with an everlasting love.**
> Jeremiah 31:3

The backpack was guaranteed for life. For life! The snaps, zippers, buckles, and straps were top of the line. Seams were triple-stitched with heavy-duty Kevlar thread. The backpack's fabric was fireproof, rip resistant, and virtually indestructible! If the backpack failed to live up to my expectations, the problem would be cheerfully fixed, or the entire backpack replaced—free of charge. Guaranteed! For life!

Along with such a fantastic lifetime guarantee, of course, came an exorbitant price. A price I was willing to pay. After all, the backpack was guaranteed. For life!

Then I read the fine print. What doesn't the guarantee cover? Dirt. That's right, dirt. Maybe I'm oversimplifying. Here's what the manufacturer actually said: "Exceptions to our guarantee: We cannot, by law, repair your backpack if excessive odor and/or filthiness are present." Huh? If I fall into a mud puddle or encounter a frightened skunk, the guarantee is voided? Maybe the guarantee isn't as great as it first sounds!

Jeremiah 31:3 spells out a different kind of guarantee—one with no exceptions. It's God's guarantee of love for you. That love will never end. Ever. There is no fine print. There are no exclusions. This exceptional guarantee hinges on one word: *everlasting*. "I have loved you with an everlasting love," God says. Paul elaborates:

For I am sure that neither death nor life, nor angels nor rulers, nor things present nor things to come, nor powers, nor height nor depth, nor anything else in all creation, will be able to separate us from the love of God in Christ Jesus our Lord.

Romans 8:38–39

Even when life gets messy, even in life's chaos and clutter, God will honor his guarantee to love you. The sudden death of a loved one will not stop God's love for you in Christ. Nor will an unplanned pregnancy. Nor will the loss of a job. Nor will a broken relationship. Nor will pain or diabetes or cancer. Nor will secret sins.

What keeps you from enjoying God's everlasting love today? Add it to the list above. It's all covered. Guaranteed! For life here on earth—and beyond! What's more, this guarantee is backed by the death and resurrection of our Savior, Jesus Christ. God's love for you is guaranteed. For life! Forever!

Help me focus on your love today, Lord Jesus . . .

What Kind of Love?

> *I have loved you with an everlasting love.*
> **Jeremiah 31:3**

What kind of love motivates a mom to help her son's Scout group tie food donation bags on every front door of every house in every subdivision in town—even when the windchill registers a brutal 11 degrees? What kind of love smiles patiently (most of the time) at the boys' antics, even though she hasn't felt her toes for over an hour?

She could have stayed in bed. It was Saturday, after all. But love compelled her. More than love, really. Commitment and determination, actually. A love committed to her young son and determined to help him learn valuable lessons about helping others. This kind of love—a determined, sacrificial commitment—is a special kind of love. In a very small way, this love helps us begin to comprehend the kind of love God has for us.

God's love lies beyond all human understanding. It's a love so deep, in fact, and so different from the love we know and experience from people around us, that it's hard to put into words.

God's love is rooted in an abiding commitment to do what is best for us. The love of God continually motivates him to work on our behalf. God's love toward us is not thwarted, does not diminish, even when we turn our backs on him and walk away. God's love compels him to draw us back . . . all the way back into his loving arms.

God's love for you—his commitment to you—demanded selfless sacrifice. That relentless love compelled him to send his Son, Jesus, into this sin-darkened world. Jesus' love for you pressed him toward the cross, there to die for you. Then, by rising from death in victory, your Savior overcame death's power and secured for you a place of welcome in God's family—forever!

This kind of absolute love changes everything for us! And it certainly also changes us at the core of our being! This love overwhelms our selfishness, purifies our motivations, and propels us to act in love for the benefit of others. We commit to love as we have been loved. And the Holy Spirit provides the power we need to do just that.

Loving Lord, your unsurpassed love is deeper and fuller than I can imagine. Forgive my selfishness, and help me to live in love more and more . . .

*I have loved you with an
everlasting love.*

Jeremiah 31:3

Stand, looking into a mirror as you say the
following words, personalizing God's love for
you in Jesus:

**God loves me. He has always loved me—
even before he gave me breath, he loved
me. God loves me with a genuine love that
will never end. No matter what happens,
nothing—nothing at all—can stop God's
love for me.**

When do you find it hardest to believe the
genuine, relentless love God has
for you in the cross of his Son?
Talk to your Lord about it
as you sketch or write in a
journal today.

Woman of God®

Living Loved ~ and Learning

eek first the kingdom of God and his righteousness.

Matthew 6:33

"To know you is to love you . . ." The group The Teddy Bears popularized those song lyrics in the late 1950s. Ever since, the lyrics have been tweaked and recorded by a variety of artists. But are the lyrics true? Can getting to know someone cause love to grow? Are knowing and loving connected somehow? Hmmm

Is it possible to more fully experience and appreciate God's love by learning more about him? We'll find out this week. Ready? Let's get started!

Ready to Learn

> **Be still, and know that I am God.**
> Psalm 46:10

Canned laughter from the game show blared from the TV and flooded through every room in the house. Occasionally, applause and raucous cheers interrupted the laughter. Fighting to stay focused on her homework, the teen glanced up at the screen every time she heard a new blast of noise. Will she finish her homework? Will she ever learn how to learn?

"All instruction in this course is online for your convenience. To log on, simply enter your student ID number, the name and number for this course, the maiden name of your great-grandmother, and the number of vowels in your street address." Okay, yes, I may have added a bit of sarcasm here. But to me, actual log-on directions make just about as much sense as my ridiculous additions. Would I ever learn how to access the course or participate in the online discussions? Would I ever learn how to learn?

Sometimes learning how to learn is half the battle. In Psalm 46:10, our Lord encourages us to "Be still" and in that stillness, get to know him. It sounds great—in theory. Get quiet and contemplate God. Stop what you're doing for a minute and get to know God better.

In reality, it's not as easy as it sounds. All kinds of things interrupt our stillness. Job pressures. Snarled traffic. Relationship stressors. Health concerns. And more besides. Be still? I really wish I could! But how?

The rest of the verse answers our questions: "Know that I am God." There's the key! I can be still, because God is God! He's in control. Totally. In. Control. I am free to relax in his arms. I can trust him to fight for me:

Casting all your anxieties on him, because he cares for you.

1 Peter 5:7

With that in mind, take a break from all the chaos of everyday life. Think about how much God loves you. Remember that he lavishes his grace and forgiveness upon you in the cross of his Son. Learn to be still so you can know—so you can be ready for what God wants to teach you.

Lord God, help me be still so that I can learn more and more about your love for me. Teach me to relax in your love. Then . . .

Learning Your Name

> **Those who know your name put their trust in you.**
> **Psalm 9:10**

Names are important. A name is more than just a simple syllable or two used to identify someone. Names have meaning—and have had since the beginning of time. The name *Eve*, for example, means "mother of all the living."

Did you know that traditionally, Native American babies were given a name at birth, but in adulthood the person frequently changed her name—perhaps because of a special accomplishment or a major lifetime event? It was common for a Native American to have several different names over the course of a lifetime. And each name helped describe more fully the person's history, character, or abilities.

Names are important. This is especially true when it comes to our triune God. His names tell us who he is, what he has done for us, and what he intends to do.

Consider *Elohim*, the first name for God the Bible uses:

In the beginning, God [Elohim] created the heavens and the earth. Genesis 1:1

Elohim is derived from a Hebrew root word that means "power" or "strength." It's impossible for us to imagine the power required or the wisdom involved in the creation of all that exists. We can only marvel—and bow in worship.

Throughout the Old Testament, *Elohim* is paired with additional words to describe the many characteristics and actions of God. For example,

The LORD is the true God; he is the living God and the everlasting King. Jeremiah 10:10

The "living God" contrasts with the false gods whom the people of that time and place worshiped. Those gods were powerless to help their adherents. But the living, powerful God, the true God who revealed himself to Abraham, to Isaac, to Jacob, is mighty to save. In love, he came again and again to help his people. In love, he comes still today to help us.

This brings us to perhaps the most precious name of all. The name *Jesus* means "the Lord saves." Living up to that name took Jesus from heaven to earth, from his eternal throne to the hill called Calvary. There he bled and died in glory—the glory of unwavering love for us.

Look back at the names of God listed above. Choose one of them, a name that brings you comfort, joy, or courage, and talk to your Savior-God today using that name.

Learning & Transformed

> **Be transformed by the renewal of your mind.**
> Romans 12:2

If you Google *transformation*, you'll get too many results to count. Many of these feature a successful dieter's before-and-after pictures. Some show the benefits of tattoo removal or permanent makeup procedures. Any room in your home can be transformed, too. Just call a professional interior decorator. Transformation is pretty popular!

The world's idea of transformation is very different from the transformation the Bible describes. Our world concentrates on changing us on the outside—the part of us that others see. Our Lord, though, is interested in transforming what's on the inside—our hearts.

Just how does this transformation happen?

All of us who have had that veil removed can see and reflect the glory of the Lord. And the Lord—who is the Spirit—makes us more and more like him as we are changed into his glorious image. 2 Corinthians 3:18 NLT

After Moses received the Ten Commandments from the Lord on Mount Sinai, his face shone with the brilliance that came from being in the presence of the holy God. In time, this brilliance gradually faded.

Today, when Christians contemplate the Lord's glory—particularly the glory of his love, revealed in Jesus our Savior—something different happens. The glory of the Lord does not fade away. Instead, the glory of Christ's love for us transforms us more and more into the image of Christ.

That's a lot to think about! How do we experience the Lord's glory? When do we stand in the Lord's presence? Whenever we read or hear God's Word, especially the Gospel message of our Savior's forgiveness and his everlasting love for us.

In those moments, the Holy Spirit works through his Word to change us—really and truly transform us from the inside out! God promises:

I will give you a new heart, and I will put a new spirit in you. I will take out your stony, stubborn heart and give you a tender, responsive heart. Ezekiel 36:26 NLT

That's powerful transformation! The more we realize God's love for us in Christ, the more our stubborn, selfish hearts soften. Then, as our hearts change, our outward lives change, too. We begin to live more and more for others. We reflect Christ's grace toward us as we share his grace and love with those around us.

Lord, as I read your Word, remind me I am in your presence. Transform me . . .

Learning
Who Is on My Side

> *This I know, that God is for me.*
> Psalm 56:9

Competition is everywhere. T-ball players feel it, and it looms large in professional locker rooms and stadiums across the world.

Competition is not confined solely to sports, though. Have you ever felt competitive at work? among your neighbors? with your family members? Sure! Coming out on top feels great! But we all know how it feels to be on the losing side, too.

At times, life itself can feel like a constant, competitive struggle. In frustration or pain, we shout out the question, "Whose side are you on?" And when we're honest, we must admit we are directing this question toward God.

The stunned mother, surveying her family's tornado-flattened home, asks, "How could this happen?" The young woman whose cancer has returned asks, "Whose side are you on, God?" The grief-stricken wife, walking back to the limousine at the cemetery, asks, "How can I live without him, Lord?"

"Whose side are you on, God?"

How can you stand tall, confident of victory, when tragedy, loss, and sorrow come crashing in? When it's life vs. me, how can "me" ever win?

When you ask questions like these, God wants you to know—to know for certain, without any doubt—that he is unconditionally on your side. Jesus once promised:

Here on earth you will have many trials and sorrows. But take heart, because I have overcome the world. John 16:33 NLT

Will faithful Christians experience setbacks? tragedies? grief? Yes. Yes. And yes. But take heart, Jesus says. This world may give us its worst, but Jesus has given us his best. His sinless life and innocent death have paid the enormous debt we had piled up by our sins. Christ's resurrection guarantees his victory (and ours) over death itself. And because it has, we can live in peace despite any defeat we ever face.

The Lord is on my side; I will not fear. Psalm 118:6

It is the Lord your God who fights for you, just as he promised you. Joshua 23:10

This I know, that God is for me. Psalm 56:9

Read those words again. And again. When the competition threatens to overpower you, when defeat seems imminent, remember: In everlasting love, the Lord is on your side.

No matter what I face today, Lord, remind me you are with me, in love, to help. Remind me . . .

Learning to Follow

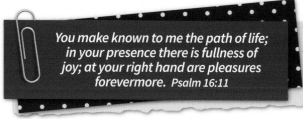

You make known to me the path of life; in your presence there is fullness of joy; at your right hand are pleasures forevermore. **Psalm 16:11**

On the park brochure, the path was labeled "Easy Hike." But recent heavy rain made much of the trail impossible to find, let alone follow. The "easy hike" turned into a grueling, five-hour trek—and we had the mud-caked boots and bruised, swollen shins to prove it.

Life is often compared to a path, a trail, a journey. The path begins at birth and comes to an end at death. All along life's path, or so the story goes, we will encounter good things and bad. We may have to scramble under branches (hardships and disappointments). We may have to clamber over rocks (challenges).

It's an interesting picture, but it isn't exactly what the psalm writer had in mind when the Holy Spirit inspired him to write these words:

You make known to me the path of life; in your presence there is fullness of joy; at your right hand are pleasures forevermore.

Psalm 16:11

One important difference between this psalm and the story people tell themselves about "life's journey" is that the path the psalmist describes has no end. We will one day live with our Lord—forever—in resurrected, glorious bodies—bodies free from sickness, free from pain. Bodies beyond the grasp of death.

What's more, believers in Christ do not walk the path of life alone. No, we walk continually in the presence of our Savior-King, the one who loves us with everlasting love. We walk along at his right hand, a position of honor. There, we enjoy the good and perfect gifts God gives:

Every good gift and every perfect gift is from above, coming down from the Father of lights with whom there is no variation or shadow due to change. James 1:17

The path of life is not really a path at all. It's a person—Jesus himself. He is the way—the only way—to eternal life. He leads, guides, protects, defends, and safely carries us to the heavenly home that even now, he's preparing for each of us:

I am the way, and the truth, and the life. No one comes to the Father except through me.
John 14:6

Lord Jesus, I commend to you every step I take . . .

The fear of the LORD is the beginning of knowledge.

Proverbs 1:7

On another sheet of paper, list all the ways you can learn more and more about your Savior, as a Woman of God: Living Loved—and Learning.

Then look back at the list you made. Place a star beside the ways you currently learn about Jesus. Pray about how you might explore more opportunities to learn, through your church, community Bible studies, online Bible courses, and more. Jot down your ideas.

Then choose one new opportunity and try it out this week.

Woman of God®

Living Loved ~ and Serving

Through love serve one another.
Galatians 5:13

Serving. There's an app for that. It's true! If you download the Goodservice app, you can access help at any time. Simply describe what needs to be done, and Goodservice will send someone to do it. Need to get flowers to a hospitalized friend? Goodservice is at your service~ for a fee, of course.

Everyone around us is so busy with work, family, and personal priorities. No one has time to serve anyone else anymore. Maybe serving one another will become obsolete. Or will it? Let's find out!

Loved to Humbly Serve

> *Jesus knew that his hour had come to depart out of this world to the Father. . . . He poured water into a basin and began to wash the disciples' feet. John 13:1–5*

Check out this list of excuses. Do any of them sound familiar?

I'd like to, but I'm really busy at work right now.

I'd like to, but I have other plans for that day/weekend/month/year.

I'd like to, but I think someone else would do a better job.

I'd like to, but I'm burned out from helping. I need a break for a while. I promised myself that I wouldn't take on any more obligations.

I'd like to, but I need to spend more time with my family.

Excuses. Sadly, we've all used them. Sometimes we do truly need to say no. But other times, our excuses are less than genuine. Sometimes they are rooted more deeply in selfishness than in reality.

Serving others sometimes seems to demand too much: too much time, too much energy, too much money. Serving others can also seem like too little: too little reward, too little recognition. Whether it's too much or too little, humble service simply doesn't always fit into our priorities.

Look again at the list of excuses. Do you notice any similarities? Every excuse begins with the word *I*. There is a connection between humility and service. Someone once wrote: "True humility is not thinking less of yourself. It's thinking of yourself less." When we put ourselves first, serving is often relegated to last place.

On the night before Jesus died, he knelt down to wash the feet of his disciples. If anyone could have offered up legitimate reasons to avoid serving, it was our Lord Jesus on that particular night. No doubt, the thought of what he was to endure in the hours ahead was overwhelming. Then, too, he was the Son of God, God himself! No one could claim such menial service was rightly his.

But surprise! Jesus doesn't make excuses. He doesn't complain or try to guilt someone else into picking up the towel. He sees dirty feet and kneels down to help. That's service. Authentic, self-forgetful service.

Lord Jesus, you died for my sinful selfishness and pride. Forgive me, and work in me a truly humble heart ~ a heart that longs to serve others in your name . . .

Loved & Glad to Serve

> **Serve the LORD with gladness!**
> **Psalm 100:2**

A popular fast-food restaurant instills an attitude of grateful service into every worker. Employees are trained to respond, "My pleasure!" whenever a customer makes a request or says, "Thank you."

This "elevated language" is intended to make interactions between customers and workers more personal and polite. Customers report that such phrases foster goodwill. Many workers feel that using this elevated language gives them, as workers, more joy in their tasks, as well.

My pleasure. Is it really possible to serve with pleasure or gladness, as Psalm 100:2 puts it? Yes! If we remember *whom* we are serving:

Worship the Lord your God, and him only shall you serve.

Luke 4:8

God in heaven doesn't need our acts of service, but the people around us do. And our service to them is "worship in work boots." Every sandwich made for a hungry person, each hug of encouragement we give to the elderly, and every winter coat we donate to the less fortunate is a way of worshiping God. Serving others honors our Lord. We worship him through even our simplest acts of service.

What's more, Jesus says that our serving, our caring for others, is in reality, showing love to him:

As you did it to one of the least of these my brothers, you did it to me. Matthew 25:40

Genuine service is not coerced or forced. A pastor friend liked to say, "I don't have to volunteer. I *get* to volunteer!" He viewed service as a real opportunity.

We must admit, though, that not all serving is easy. Sometimes helping and loving others is hard work—really hard. Sometimes those we serve are not thankful. They may even criticize. But God's everlasting love for us, love demonstrated on the cross where Christ died for us, keeps us going. It makes our service exciting, even when others try our patience.

With worship as our focus, and loving Jesus as our intention, our acts of service for others become truly freeing experiences. We are free to worship our God and all he has done for us through his Son, our Savior. We gladly love and serve, optimizing the opportunities God provides. Serving others becomes a blessing to us, and our true pleasure!

I praise you, Lord, for all you've done for me. Help me worship you by . . .

Loved & Compelled to Serve

> *The love of Christ controls us . . . that those who live might no longer live for themselves but for him who for their sake died and was raised.* **2 Corinthians 5:14–15**

"What motivates you?" If you've been on many job interviews, you have probably answered that question at least once. Many job-finder websites offer advice on ways to ace this question. These sites also urge job applicants to practice their answer before they step into the interviewer's office.

Why do prospective employers want to know what motivates you? Your answer helps them better understand your personality, it gives them an idea of how well you'll fit into the company's culture, and it hints at what they can expect from you when the boss begins handing out assignments.

Some motivators are positive, and some are negative. The opportunity to earn more money, chances for advancement, and the potential for public recognition are all positive motivators. Negative motivators are most often rooted in fear: fear of failure, loss of prestige, bankruptcy, or a shredded reputation.

So what motivates Christians to serve others in authentic love? Money, fame, and awards rarely result from humble service. Negative motivators can't play a part in Christian service either. We have no fear of judgment or death. Our good works will not, cannot earn God's favor; that favor is already ours because of what Jesus did for us:

By grace you have been saved through faith. And this is not your own doing; it is the gift of God, not a result of works. Ephesians 2:8–9

As believers in Christ, our future is secure. It is sealed in the life, death, and resurrection of our Savior, Jesus. The Bible explains our certain hope:

You also, when you heard the word of truth, the gospel of your salvation, and believed in him, were sealed with the promised Holy Spirit. Ephesians 1:13

What then drives Christians to help others? The words of 2 Corinthians 5:14–15 sum up the answer. When Christ lives in our hearts by faith, the Holy Spirit begins his transformative work in us. Prompted by him, we begin to see others in light of what our Savior did for them, as well as for us. We are compelled, driven to serve because of Christ's everlasting love.

Holy Spirit, help me recognize opportunities to serve others today . . .

Loved to Freely Serve

> For you were called to freedom, brothers.
> Only do not use your freedom as an
> opportunity for the flesh, but through
> love serve one another. Galatians 5:13

"No more teachers! No more books! . . . " When summer vacation arrives, most school-age children relish their newfound freedom. They envision glorious, lazy days at the pool, sleeping until noon, and doing whatever they want for three whole months! Now that's freedom!

Why, then, not two weeks into summer break, do moms often hear the plaintive cry, "I'm bored! There's nothing to do!"

Or consider the retiree who says, "I've worked toward this for decades! I'm so happy to leave my assignments to someone else. Retirement, here I come!" Freedom to come and go at will. No schedule to follow. No responsibilities. That's freedom! Or is it?

Countless rounds of golf, two dozen tennis lessons,

and three cruises on low-cost-drop-everything-last-minute travel junkets later, we hear the same retiree sigh, "I feel so useless. What's the point of even getting up in the morning?"

Freedom. It sounds great. You may be thinking, "I'd like to try it! I could use more freedom in my life! Freedom wouldn't be wasted on me! No way!" But in reality, freedom easily becomes a new kind of prison, because we tend to turn the blessing of freedom into the bonds of selfishness. Freedom can truly become a new kind of slavery, if we use our freedom solely for ourselves.

So, what then? How can we properly use the hard-fought freedom Christ won for us on his cross? Through loving service! Serving others moves the focus of our freedom outward. Through the eyes of Christ, we see in our freedom limitless opportunities to serve our Lord by serving others.

The good news is that we don't need to wait until school ends or retirement begins! Opportunities for humble service are waiting for us right now. Ask your family and extended family for ways you can serve them. Check out your church's newsletter or bulletin board. Inquire at your local food bank, Red Cross, or nursing home. Research local schools and the Salvation Army. Check websites like www.volunteermatch. com and others. Pray. Then pick a project and use your freedom to serve.

Thank you, Jesus, for the freedom you won for me. Help me use my freedom wisely. Show me how I can best honor you . . .

Loved & Wired for Service

> *We are his workmanship, created in Christ Jesus for good works, which God prepared beforehand, that we should walk in them. Ephesians 2:10*

Can you get fresh coffee out of a toaster? No! How about cold milk from the oven? Ridiculous! Will a car launder your clothing? Preposterous! Toasters are made for browning bread and bagels. Ovens are wired to heat, not cool. And your best bet for clean laundry is a washing machine. It was created for just that purpose.

How something is invented, wired, or created determines how it works. How something is invented, wired, or created determines its purpose. Simple, right? Well what about you? What were you created—uniquely—to do?

To find the answer, you first need to ask the right questions. Who created you? God did. How did he do that? Your Lord called you into being with gentle, but purposeful intent:

You formed my inward parts; you knitted me together in my mother's womb. Psalm 139:13

This passage makes one thing clear: our Creator uses no cookie cutters, no assembly lines. We are "formed," "knitted," one-of-a-kind creations.

So what is it that God has fashioned you to do? Think about your relationships. Are you a neighbor, friend, daughter, sister, or mother? Think about your personality. Are you wired to be an understanding listener or an objective thinker or the good-natured, quick-with-a-joke co-worker everyone invites to parties? Think about your talents. Has God designed you to be an inquisitive scientist? a cordial customer-relations expert? a sensitive counselor? a knowledgeable instructor?

Ephesians 2:10 describes the purposes God has in mind for you. Read it again—aloud and slowly. Wow! We are created for service—good works. Our Creator has had these specific things in mind just for us since the day he called us into being!

Note that we are "created in Christ." No longer our original, sinful selves, through faith in our Savior, we are the redeemed children of God. We reflect his holy, perfect, image to others. Our works of service are not our own. They, too, have become God's workmanship—his work—through our willing, serving hands. What's more, there's this:

He who began a good work in you will bring it to completion at the day of Jesus Christ.

Philippians 1:6

Lord Jesus, as I read these words, many thoughts are stirring in my heart . . .

> *Worship the Lord your God, and him*
> *only shall you serve.*
>
> Luke 4:8

Genuine, grateful service. What images do these words bring to your mind? How do they apply to your life right now? How might they continue to apply in the weeks and years to come?

Jot down your thoughts on a piece of paper. Then talk to your Savior about ways he would have you worship and serve him as you serve others here on earth.

Woman of God®

Living Loved ~ and Loving

Loving can be easy. It can also be difficult. Very difficult. How do you show love to someone who has hurt you~over and over again? Loving the unlovable is challenging at best. Even loving yourself can seem both indulgent and absolutely necessary at the same time.

So how can love serve as a blueprint for my life? Perhaps this week's devotional thoughts will help clarify what God is saying to us in 1 John 4:8.

Anyone who does not love does not know God, because God is love.

1 John 4:8

Loved & Loving Still

> *Do not be anxious about anything, but in everything by prayer and supplication with thanksgiving let your request be made known to God.* **Philippians 4:6**

We stood in line, waiting to check out. It was the Express Lane, but obviously in name only. In front of me stood three other customers. We waited our turns, but the line simply was not moving.

The man in front of me anxiously looked at his watch. Three times. Then he abruptly wrenched his cart to the left and made a bee line for a different lane.

The woman who now stood second in line in front of me glanced at her phone, checking the time. Quickly reconsidering her two purchases, she glanced at me apologetically. Then she placed her items—a tube of mascara and small box of eyeshadow colors—on the shelf between the candy bars and mint gum and left the store. Time is more valuable than beauty, I smiled.

No matter. Because now I was next!

That's when I noticed her—the elderly woman just checking out. She wore support hosiery and black, sensible shoes under her faded print dress. The clerk smiled, handing her a small bag. "See you tomorrow!" the clerk said, as the customer walked away. Then, in a hushed voice, she confided, "She comes in almost every day. I think she's lonely."

As my items bleep across the price scanner, I'm thinking: lonely. She's lonely. I'm in a big, big hurry, but she's lonely. Suddenly my priorities are reshuffled and straightened out. My frustration at having to wait fades. I smile. Love is more important than time.

Everyone has the same 24 hours each day. That's 1,440 minutes or 86,400 seconds! Put that way, there seems to be a lot of time. How long did it take the clerk to share a little love with that woman? A minute? Probably less. How do some people actually find the time to show love? It's a matter of priorities.

But when so many people need love—especially the love that Christ offers—how do we decide when and how to love all those around us? When we ask Jesus to point out the opportunities, he will! The one who died in everlasting love for you will teach you to slow down and take time to love.

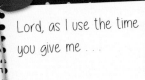

Lord, as I use the time you give me . . .

Loved & Forgiven to Love Others

> *A new commandment I give to you, that you love one another: just as I have loved you.*
> John 13:34

Who is it in your life? The ever-critical mother-in-law? The bully boss? The neighborhood gossip? The fraudster who conned away your hard-earned savings? who seems impossible to love? Does God expect you to love that person? Really?

Our Lord answered that question in the Upper Room the night before he died. Supper was over. The Last Supper. Judas had run from the room, outed by the Savior whom he would soon betray. The stunned disciples raised their confused gazes to meet Jesus' eyes. There, they saw no disgust, no hatred. Only compassion and love.

Love? Love for the betrayer, Judas? Perplexed, the disciples listened in disbelief to what Jesus said next:

A new commandment I give to you, that you love one another: just as I have loved you. John 13:34

It's a commandment, not a suggestion. But how? How can we who have been bruised and broken, disgraced and even ruined by the thoughtless—and sometimes deliberate—words and actions of others still love like Jesus loves?

A good place to begin, perhaps, is to consider Jesus' everlasting love for us. He loves us in our better moments and when we're at our most unlovable. Jesus loves us. Period. Completely. Without hesitation. He loved us to death—his own—and he continues to love us: deeply, genuinely, perfectly.

That love is the source of all love. Jesus makes it possible for us to become a kind of "love pipeline" through which his personal, priceless love can flow into the lives of those who have hurt us so much.

Our Savior's love will also help us put our feelings aside in order to pray for others, even those whose words and actions have wounded us deeply. Touched and healed by his grace, we can ask our Lord to forgive them, bless them, and yes, even prosper them:

You have heard that it was said, "You shall love your neighbor and hate your enemy." But I say to you, Love your enemies and pray for those who persecute you. Matthew 5:43–44

Our spite, and even our hatred, has been forgiven. That makes it possible for us to forgive and to go on loving—just like Jesus!

Jesus, help me tear up the IOUs I'm holding, especially . . .

Loved & Loving Consistently

"It looks good on you," the salesperson gushed. "The style! The color! The fit! Everything about it is just perfect!"

Perfect! That's how my week was going. And really, I silently mused, the past several weeks have been pretty perfect, too! Stepping up to the cash register to pay, I heard my phone. The new, upbeat ringtone made me smile. But my smile didn't last. Thank heavens for caller ID!

I wasn't going to ruin my perfectly perfect day by listening to my friend complain about her life—again! Setting the phone to "I'm busy. I'll call you later." I quickly dropped it back into my purse and returned my attention to my purchase. Smiling, I left the store, humming a tune all the way to my car.

Fastening my seatbelt, I reconsidered the phone call from my friend. Lord, how can I love when "I'm ok, but you're a mess"? How can I be compassionate to the downhearted, when I'm feeling on top of the world?

We've all probably wondered that at times. Showing love in those kinds of circumstances is not easy. Honestly, it's impossible! Until, that is, we remember who we are. Just think! You are God's chosen one, made holy through the cross of Christ. The sinless Son of God himself died for you! You are loved beyond words and blessed beyond imagination.

Along with his forgiveness, God has given you compassion—it's already hanging there in the closet of your heart—a gift from your heavenly Father. Kindness is there in the closet, too—an unselfish and gentle spirit. And humility. It's on the rack there next to meekness—both inspiring self-forgetful concern for others. Finally, there's patience, the ability to put up with the faults of others, cheerfully sharing their burdens.

The Bible invites us to put these things on, just like a new outfit. We need compassion, kindness, humility, meekness, and patience so much more than we need new shoes or a new dress for work. And they are ours—free! All from our Lord.

Lord Jesus, go ahead! Totally outfit me! Wrap your cloak of love around my shoulders. Take off my selfish attitudes and give me your brand of love . . .

Loved & Genuinely Loving

> *Let love be genuine.*
> Romans 12:9

Does the name Eddie Haskell ring a bell? Eddie was Wally Cleaver's best friend on the television sitcom *Leave It to Beaver.* Although the show ended in 1963, you can still catch the reruns today and witness Eddie's shallow ethics and questionable character.

Eddie was known for his insincerity. The Beaver branded him "a real weasel." All the characters on the show had trouble liking Eddie, probably because of their overwhelming suspicions that even while Eddie was complimenting them, he was plotting against them!

Insincerity didn't end in 1963. It's alive and well today!

Take for example, the worker who generously praises her boss at the office, but can't find anything good to say about the boss to her family at home.

Or consider the generous donor to the homeless shelter who gives only because she needs a sizable tax deduction.

We are all at times tempted to show love to others solely because of the benefit we ourselves will receive in return. This kind of backhanded, insincere, and self-serving love is just the opposite of the love God wants to see in our lives. He wants our love to be genuine. Real, not faked. Honest, not false. Our Savior wants us to have a genuine and unselfish love, a love offered freely, no strings attached!

How can you distinguish real love from its selfish counterfeit?

You shall love your neighbor as yourself. James 2:8

Few of us have trouble loving ourselves. We do most of what we do each day for our own benefit. Loving ourselves is ridiculously easy for most. How can we transfer this kind of love to others?

We can't. Not on our own. If we are going to live lives of unselfish commitment to the welfare of others, we need our Savior to work that in us. Jesus' love is the only absolutely genuine love. It's the love that bled and died for us!

Authentic love starts with repentance. Ask Jesus to forgive the times your "love" was only a way of getting what you wanted. Ask him to help you recognize when your love for others is only selfishness in disguise. Your Savior can and will change your love. He will make it real!

I want genuine love, Lord Jesus. Make it real, like yours is real . . .

Loved & Forever Loving

> **I trust in the steadfast love of God forever and ever.**
> **Psalm 52:8**

Maybe you've seen it? The mirage on the highway or in the gully just ahead in the heat of summer? It tricks your eyes into thinking that an oasis, a river, a lake filled with cool water lies directly in your path and not all that far away.

But when you arrive at the point where the lake should be, you find nothing but hot asphalt or burning sand. The mirage has moved! Now the lake lies just ahead of you again, tempting you to chase it. No matter how fast you travel, you'll never catch up to the mirage. It will remain forever elusive, always just out of reach.

The Samaritan woman described in John 4:4–30, may well have believed she was chasing mirages. She had chalked up several failed marriages and was now, again, living with a man, though they were not married.

As she made her daily trip to collect water from the well, she was thirsty. Not so much for water but for genuine love. For forgiveness and acceptance. Her hard life had not hardened her heart, not completely.

Jesus knew all of the above. He knew of her thirst. That's why he waited for her at the well. He wanted to offer her more than she could have imagined—living water. The forgiveness and mercy of God. A place to belong in his family. His own everlasting love.

Jesus freely offered it to her. He offers it to you, as well! The love that your Lord has for you never fails. It is constant. Eternal. Nothing you have done or could ever do disqualifies you from receiving his love. Absolutely nothing! Your every sin has been crossed out—forgiven through Christ's cross.

Let that sink in: Jesus loves you! He always has and he always will. He has made you part of God's family through faith. You belong to him!

The living water is no mirage. You don't need to chase after it. Your Savior showers it on you freely:

See how very much our Father loves us, for he calls us his children, and that is what we are!
1 John 3:1 NLT

Lord Jesus, I am thirsty. Quench my need for joy and peace in your everlasting love today, especially . . .

*Let me hear in the morning of your steadfast love,
for in you I trust. Make me know the way I
should go, for to you I lift up my soul.*

Psalm 143:8

Your love for me, Lord, makes me want to love
those around me more fully, more unconditionally.
When I notice the ways your love touches and
heals my life, the Holy Spirit compels me to
share your overwhelming, everlasting love and
joy with others.

Where do I begin, Lord?
Impress upon my heart
the ways you would
have me show your
love today and every
day. In Jesus' name.
Amen.

Woman of God®

Living Loved~ Forever

*I trust in you, O LORD;
I say, "You are my
God." My times are
in your hand.*

Psalm 31:14~15

Time is measured in seconds, minutes, and hours. It's also measured in days, weeks, months, and years. Sometimes, though, we measure time by what's happening in our lives. We call them the "times" or "seasons" in our life~a season of joy or a time of loss.

It's so comforting to know that no matter what "time" we find ourselves in, God's love for us remains the same. It does not change with our circumstances. We can confidently trust the God who holds us close~always.

So what "time" is it for you? This week, we'll explore the truth that your Savior's everlasting love surrounds you all the time and at all times.

Loving *When Joyful*

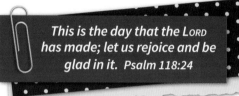

> This is the day that the LORD has made; let us rejoice and be glad in it. **Psalm 118:24**

Whoo-hoo! This day couldn't be any better! Everything—and I mean everything—is great! I feel like jumping for joy—literally! Whoo-hoo!

When is the last time you felt unbridled joy like that? The kind of elation that is impossible to fake—or reign in? The smile that lasts for so long, it makes your face hurt?

It's a fabulous feeling! Endorphins pump into your system overtime, and your heart and soul beat to the same song of joy. It's wonderful! But . . . is it right? I mean, is it okay to feel so joyful when there is so much pain and suffering in our world? What does God think of my joy?

These questions remind me of a picture created by Willis Wheatley, a Canadian artist. In the picture, Wheatley shows Jesus laughing. I can't hold back my smile when I see this picture. In it, Jesus' head is tipped back. His eyes are pinched almost shut with delight. Jesus' mouth is curved into a genuine, wide smile, and he looks as if he's ready to roar with laughter. It's a great picture, one that brings me joy!

Jesus laughing? We don't usually think of our Savior like this. Jesus came to earth on a serious mission. Conquering sin and Satan was certainly no laughing matter. The Bible tells us that Jesus wept (Luke 19:41; John 11:35), but it never mentions him laughing.

As the true human being he was, Jesus certainly would have experienced joy. He certainly shared in the elation of the blind who received sight and in the excitement of those, once lame, who left his presence dancing in delight! Jesus, our Savior, came to reclaim the joy that sin had stolen away. His death and glorious resurrection have secured our joy forever!

And if we need more proof, we have Jesus' own words:

These things I have spoken to you, that my joy may be in you, and that your joy may be full. John 15:11

That's it! Our joy—all of our joy—is rooted in our Savior's everlasting love. We can bask in that joy now, even as we look forward to its fullness in the courts of heaven.

Thank you, Jesus, for the joy your everlasting love brings into my life . . .

Loving When Lonely

> **I am with you always.**
> Matthew 28:20

Loneliness is a strange phenomenon. You can feel lonely because you are all alone—deserted and all by yourself. However, you can also feel lonely when surrounded by a huge crowd of people.

No one likes feeling lonely, and some scientists say that feelings of isolation, or loneliness, can impact your physical as well as your mental health. Studies have shown that loneliness can increase a person's mortality rate by as much as 26%.

Loneliness hurts. Just ask the newly widowed member of your church or the elderly woman confined to her bed in a nursing home. Ask the college student, so far from home, who hasn't yet made any friends. Or the recently divorced mom who feels the crushing pressure to keep things going—all by herself. Loneliness hurts. Deeply.

It's difficult to feel loved when you're feeling lonely. In fact, loneliness often starts when another person's love for you is withdrawn or withheld. But God's love is different. The love God has for you is not simply a feeling—it's so much more than that! God's love took on a tangible form for you. Love came for you in the person of Jesus Christ.

Just look at what your Savior's love prompted him to do—for you! He left his heavenly home and set aside his glory to take on human flesh. Living here on earth as a true human being, Jesus kept God's Law perfectly in your place. All because he loves you!

Then, Jesus died a criminal's death for your sins on what should have been your cross. At last, he sealed you in his love forever by rising from the dead, victorious. Even now, he continues to love you with everlasting love!

This love is active, a tangible asset you can tap into whenever you feel lonely. Jesus' love surrounds you. You are forever cherished and loved!

Next time you feel lonely, turn loneliness on its head. Use your lonely times to reflect on Jesus and on his enduring love for you. Worship him! Then think about the family of believers to which you belong. Thank God for making you part of this family. Watch for the lonely among them, and step up to encourage them with the security of Christ's unending love.

Lord, I pray for those who are lonely . . .

Loving When Experiencing Loss

> **Surely he has borne our griefs and carried our sorrows.**
> Isaiah 53:4

What have you lost? really lost? (Car keys don't count.) Think about major losses, like losing the job you had for 22 years or losing a husband after 43 years of togetherness. Think of losses that shake even the strongest faith, like the loss of watching your child painfully die from a disease that has no cure. Or consider the loss of your good reputation, the death of a cherished pet, the loss of good health.

All significant losses like these challenge even faith-filled Christians, perhaps especially faith-filled Christians.

At times of loss, Satan stands close at hand, poised and ready to jump into the void the loss leaves behind. His tactics are predictable. He may taunt you with "What ifs." He may bring up your past mistakes and sins. He may goad you with the question "Why would your God do this to you?"

Loss hurts. No one else can know exactly how much it hurts. No one else really knows how deep the hurt goes. No one—except Jesus.

Jesus experienced loss. He really did. Joseph, our Lord's earthly father, likely died before Jesus began his ministry. Jesus' own relatives and hometown friends rejected him and tried, at least once, to kill him! When his close friend Lazarus died, Jesus cried openly and without shame. One of Jesus' twelve closest friends betrayed him—for only a few silver coins! And worst of all, while suffering on his cross, Jesus experienced the devastating loss of his heavenly Father's presence. Yes, your Savior knew the pain of crushing loss.

Jesus knows the pain your losses bring, too. Your Savior wants you to know that he is grieving alongside you. He is your friend, and he wants to draw you close and envelop you in his love. No matter how long or how deeply you grieve, Jesus is there for you. He is with you and he will help you!

So long as we live in this world, we will know pain and loss. But one day, all your losses will come to a glorious and permanent end. Jesus promises:

In the world you will have tribulation. But take heart; I have overcome the world.
John 16:33

O Lord, when I experience loss, remind me to turn to you, lean on you, trust in you . . .

Loving When Experiencing Success

> *Let not steadfast love and faithfulness forsake you; bind them around your neck; write them on the tablet of your heart. So you will find favor and good success in the sight of God and man.* **Proverbs 3:3–4**

How do you define success? A hefty bank account? A big home in a prestigious neighborhood? Is success measured by acquiring education, power, or fame? If you raise successful children or grandchildren, is your life a success?

Most dictionaries define success something like this: the accomplishment of a goal or purpose. So then, it seems as though setting the right goal or knowing your purpose is critical to success.

But what about, for example, actors who study their craft, work very hard, and make it to the top, only to become addicted to drugs and alcohol? Are they successful?

Or what about the woman who breaks through all the glass ceilings in her corporation, only to find her husband and family have gone their own way? Is she a success?

Rather than accepting the definitions of success our society offers, we do well to think about how our Lord defines success:

Let not steadfast love and faithfulness forsake you; bind them around your neck; write them on the tablet of your heart. So you will find favor and good success in the sight of God and man.

Proverbs 3:3–4

These words don't seem to fit any current popular definitions. They warn us that success does not necessarily come from hard work and perseverance. It does not come from great wealth, talent, or fame. Instead, our Lord invites us to aim at two goals: love and faithfulness. What kind of success is that?!

It's godly success—and it's enduring! Fame. Wealth. Trophies. Diplomas. All fade away, fall apart, cease to matter. But Jesus, the faithful friend, who died for us, loves us with everlasting, steadfast love. When our relationship with him comes first, then our life is a success—no matter what else we have or do.

Lord, help me evaluate my life using the standards you provide. You are faithful to me. Your love is steadfast, everlasting. Teach me to prize true faithfulness and love as I . . .

Loving & Discovering Contentment

> **I have learned how to be content with whatever I have.**
> Philippians 4:11 NLT

Maybe you've heard the joke about the miser who tried to take a suitcase full of gold bars into heaven. St. Peter met him at the gate and insisted on checking the bag to see what worldly possessions were too precious to leave behind. When St. Peter opened the suitcase and saw the gold bars, he scratched his head, and in a puzzled voice exclaimed, "You brought pavement?!"

We laugh, because the joke captures our desperate attachment to earthly wealth. We see the silliness of it. The story illustrates the truth: "You can't take it with you."

Contentment is not a virtue in our competitive culture. Ads drive us to want things we didn't even know existed. And as soon as we purchase the latest, greatest thing, an even better version comes along to eclipse it! We envy friends and neighbors who live in better homes, drive fancier cars, and seem to live better lives than we do.

Comparing ourselves to others plants the seeds of jealousy and covetousness deep in our hearts. We sense that contentment would bring true peace to our lives. But how can we attain it—and keep it? How do we become truly content?

Consider thinking about contentment in a new way—as the spiritual gift from God it truly is:

Satisfy us each morning with your unfailing love, so we may sing for joy to the end of our lives. Psalm 90:14 NLT

That sounds a lot like contentment, doesn't it? Now, think about these words of our Savior:

Don't worry about anything; instead, pray about everything. Tell God what you need, and thank him for all he has done. Then you will experience God's peace, which exceeds anything we can understand. His peace will guard your hearts and minds as you live in Christ Jesus. Philippians 4:6–7 NLT

God loves you! He has always loved you! He will always love you! Confess to him the contentment-killing sins of jealousy and worry. Thank him for the forgiveness Jesus won for you on Calvary's cross. Ask him to help you trust that he will provide for you in the very best ways. Then invite the Holy Spirit to give you genuine peace.

Lord Jesus, in you—and only in you—is true contentment found. Keep me focused on your everlasting love for me . . .

I the LORD do not change.
Malachi 3:6

God's love is the only enduring constant in our ever-changing lives. Think back to a challenging time or circumstance in your past. How did God prove himself faithful to you during that time? How might remembering the past prepare you for what may lie ahead?

Is there a Bible verse from this week that touched your heart in a new way? Try committing the verse to memory.

No matter what season of life you are in right now, God's love for you is as strong as ever!

Lord God, my Savior, your love is amazing!

Help me accept and cherish the endless love you have for me.

By your powerful love, continue to equip and inspire me to love others as you make me more and more like you. Transform my love to be actionable and real~not self-serving. Help me love those around me with the kind of sacrificial love you showed for me on Calvary.

And when it's hard to love other people, when it's difficult even to love myself, remind me of your awesome love. I eagerly await the day when, with the ones I love, I will see you face-to-face, and finally, fully understand what real love looks like.

Hold me safely in your arms until that day. In Jesus' name.

amen

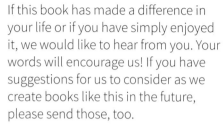

If this book has made a difference in your life or if you have simply enjoyed it, we would like to hear from you. Your words will encourage us! If you have suggestions for us to consider as we create books like this in the future, please send those, too.

Send e-mail to editor@CTAinc.com and include the subject line: WOG7SC

Write to Editorial Manager,
Department WOG7SC
CTA, Inc.
PO Box 1205
Fenton, MO 63026-1205

Or leave a product review at
www.CTAinc.com (search WOG7SC)